Knock Knock, Jingle Jingle!

{Christmas Jokes for Kids}

Brenda Ponnay

Knock! Knock! Who's there?

Ho-ho.

Ho-ho who?

Hmmmm... Your Santa impression could use a little work.

eISBN: 978-1-5324-2980-4
Paperback ISBN: 978-1-5324-2984-2
Hardcover ISBN: 978-1-5324-2988-0

Published in the United States by Xist Publishing
www.xistpublishing.com
24200 Southwest Freeway #402-290 Rosenberg, TX 77471

What is the wettest kind of animal in Santa's workshop?

Rain-deer.

What do snowmen like to do on the weekend?

Just chill out.

Knock! Knock!
Who's there?
Hanna.
Hanna who?

…*Hanna Partridge
in a pear tree!*

What kind of Christmas present just can't be beat?

A broken drum!

Knock! Knock!
Who's there?
Mary and Abbey.
Mary and Abbey who?

Mary Christmas and Abbey New Year!

What did the peanut butter say to the grape on Christmas?

"'Tis the season to be jelly!"

What do reindeer hang on their Christmas trees?

Horn-aments.

What do you call a grumpy reindeer?

Bah Humbug.

Rude-olph

Knock! Knock!
Who's there?
Snow.
Snow who?

Snowbodies there!

What do you call a snow monster that has a six-pack?

The Abdominal Snowman.

Where do snowmen go to dance?

A snow ball!

Knock, knock.
Who's there?
Doughnut
Doughnut who?

Doughnut open until Christmas Day!

What's red, white and blue
at Christmas time?

A sad candy cane!

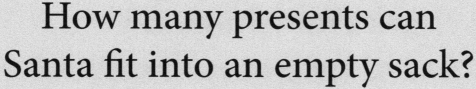

How many presents can
Santa fit into an empty sack?

Only one.
After that it's not
empty anymore.

What kind of photos do elves take?

Elfies!

What's the weather report for Christmas Eve?

There's a 100 percent chance of reindeer.

Why are Christmas trees bad at sewing?

Because they always drop their needles!

Knock! Knock!
Who's there?

Irish.
Irish who?

Irish you a Merry Christmas!

Why is it so cold at Christmas time?

Because it's Decembrrrrr.

About the Author

Brenda Ponnay is the author and illustrator of several children's books, including the popular Little Hoo series and several joke books. She lives in Southern California with her family.

Learn more about Brenda and her books at brendaponnay.com

 brendaponnay_books

Check out Brenda Ponnay's other joke books:

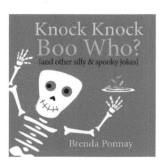

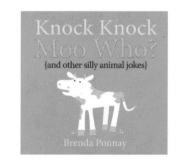

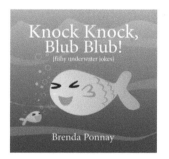

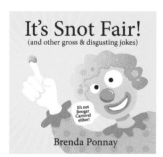

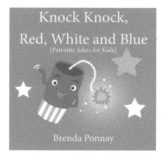